Turning
to
the
Sunset

Turning
to
the
Sunset

Poems
Barbara Berkenfield

Drawings
Susan Berkenfield

SUNSTONE
PRESS

SANTA FE

Sunstone books may be purchased for educational, business, or sales promotional use.
For information please write: Special Markets Department, Sunstone Press,
P.O. Box 2321, Santa Fe, New Mexico 87504-2321.

Book and Cover design ༈ Vicki Ahl
Body typeface ༈ Bell MT
Printed on acid free paper

Library of Congress Cataloging-in-Publication Data

Berkenfield, Barbara, 1935-
Turning to the sunset : poems / Barbara Berkenfield.
        p. cm.
ISBN 978-0-86534-827-1 (softcover : alk. paper)
I. Title.
PS3602.E7566T87 2011
811'.6--dc22

                                2011019280

WWW.SUNSTONEPRESS.COM
SUNSTONE PRESS / POST OFFICE BOX 2321 / SANTA FE, NM 87504-2321 /USA
(505) 988-4418 / ORDERS ONLY (800) 243-5644 / FAX (505) 988-1025

To Susan and Suzanne

Beloved daughters-in-law

CONTENTS

Preface   9
Prologue   13

REFLECTIONS

Ode to Eliseo and Paula_____ 17
November Night _____ 18
Dinner Conversation _____ 20
The Road to Fort Sumner _____ 22
Waiting for Baby _____ 24
Small Treasures_____ 25
Oil Spill _____ 26
Come Home Aubrey _____ 28
The Weavers of Las Golondrinas__ 29
Waiting for Work_____ 30
The Bookmark_____ 31

EARTH CONNECTIONS

Winter Sunset _____ 35
Tehachapi Pass_____ 36
Spring Green _____ 37
Summer Storm_____ 38
Forest Trail _____ 39
January End of Days_____ 41
In Between the Lines_____ 42
The Garden _____ 43
Pictures for Mom_____ 44
Christmas Road Trip_____ 46
Alameda Seasons _____ 51

PHOTO MEMORIES

Sea of Flowers _____ 55
The Valentine _____ 56
Friendship _____ 57
A Summer Day _____ 58
A Warm Day in November _____ 59

AGING

Faux Spring _____ 63
Remembering _____ 65
Family Chain _____ 68
Skin _____ 69
View from a Hammock _____ 70
Anniversary _____ 71
The Dinner Party _____ 72
Secret Thoughts _____ 73

CODA

Coda _____ 79

Preface
More Last Words

My earliest writing experience was a painful one, when my first grade teacher rapped my knuckles with her ruler for using my left hand. However I persevered and struggled to make my script letters slant as correctly as those of my classmates. Ironically, when I stood at a blackboard, I was more comfortable writing with my right hand. I still wonder how we all survived the clouds of chalk we produced while banging the felt erasers at the end of the day.

I discovered that I could write backwards with my left hand, and amazed friends and families with the stories I wrote which they had to read in a mirror. I loved all the physical accoutrements of writing and the distinctive smells of new pencils, erasers, notebooks and sticks of chalk. It seemed that we diagrammed thousands of sentences in grammar school, and the importance of good writing continued through high school.

I had family role models and teachers with creative outlets who inspired me. I took my first creative writing and poetry courses in college where we were all in love with our poet-in-residence Richard Wilbur. I began to write a few poems for a personal outlet; but it was not until we moved to France that I began to keep a yearly journal, and saw my first by-line when invited to write for the American community newspaper.

I continued to have the occasional article or poem published when we returned to the States, though it was not until we moved to Santa Fe in 1989 that I began to think of writing as a serious endeavor.

I am convinced that the creative energies of this town contributed to my achievements in this area, both with feature writing and my poetry. I often wonder if these books would exist if we had not moved here.

When my first book of poetry, Driving Toward the Moon, was published in 2005, my 70th birthday was approaching and I joked that there were not enough years remaining to write enough poems for a second volume. But my folder of new poems kept expanding over the next three years, resulting in The Earth Behind my Thumb in 2008. Its preface was titled "A Few Last Words," because surely I was finished.

Yet ruminations about personal and world events began to percolate, and my folder expanded once again. This time, the road was bumpier with more obstacles and distractions; and finding the right words to be good messengers seemed to take longer. However, by mid-2010, I decided a third book was a possibility.

Just as I wrote in my first book, I continue to pull off the road, stop in front of the bananas, set down a spatula, or get up in the night to find my note pad and write down words that are humming in my head. Inspiration still comes at the most unexpected times, and it remains those first words that are often the best and I must not lose them.

Like the format of my other two books, the poems are grouped by theme headings. In this one, the poems are organized chronologically within each theme section. The sections are introduced by the decorative drawings of my daughter-in-law Susan Berkenfield.

—Barbara Berkenfield
Santa Fe, New Mexico, 2011

Prologue

Turning to the Sunset

Three quarters of a century,
Another milestone met.
The road ahead gets shorter.
The road behind
Filled now with memories
Of family, love, children's embraces,
Grandchildren's hugs.

Childhood, college, New York years,
A decade in France and
Travels far and near.
Now two decades
At home in Santa Fe.

My thoughts are ready
To share with you
In this last chapter,
As I reflect about today,
And recall the past
With old photos,
Letters, friends
Before turning
To the sunset.

November 8, 2010
75th Birthday, Santa Fe, New Mexico

REFLECTIONS

Ode to Eliseo and Paula

They left this life
Four months apart.
At ninety three she led the way
From the home they built in Santa Fe.

A couple made in heaven
But, unlike Adam and Eve,
Were never expelled
From their garden,
A place of devotion, art, and family.

Inspirational and pure of heart
Their garden and their family
Grew with the passing years,
As they revived straw appliqué traditions.

Mentors to Hispanic artists
On their own paths to tradition,
Their creativity unfolded
Like a flower in the sun.

Small and unassuming,
Devoted to each other,
They left giant footprints
On our New Mexico land
And the world beyond.

April 2009
Eliseo and Paula Rodriguez were both artists of traditional Spanish
straw appliqué—a medium they raised to new levels of complexity
and creativity. Long time Spanish Market artists, they became Santa
Fe Living Treasures in 1998, and in 2004 were named National
Endowment of the Arts National Heritage Fellows.

November Night

Autumn light was fading
When acres of Grant Park
Began to fill,
An extraordinary carpet
Of people of all races, all places.

Shoulder to shoulder
Together for hours
They gave each other warmth
In the evening chill,
United in the belief
That he would win.

Before this sea of people
He stood in the media glow
To bring us the gift
Of hope for the future
Of our children.

Filled with thanks,
We wished to live long enough
To be part of his future
With hopes of recovery
From the eight years past,
When a time of selfish direction
Sent us to a drear despair of debt.

Countless challenges he faces
To rescue us from doubt,
Division and derision,
And return us to the country
The world thought
Might not be strong again.

That night we shouted
In celebration,
Secure in the knowledge,
Despite the gauntlets thrown,
He would bring reason,
Understanding and patience
To our side.

November 4, 2008

Dinner Conversation

Eli is sad.
Willow died.
She wasn't nice,
His Nana's old dog.

At dinner
Eli's chin is trembly.
His mouth looks funny,
Turned upside down
Like a horseshoe.

He asks Daddy
Lots of questions.
His eyes are teary.

Do people die?
Can you talk
After you die?
Can you walk?
Will I die tomorrow?
The next day?
More than a year?

A hundred years
Says Daddy
Don't worry so.

Eli gives a little smile,
Looks at his plate.
I am not going to eat
Those beans!
Just two more bites
Says Daddy.
Eli is happy now.

Sam is listening
But he is not sad,
Because he is in his 'magination,
Fighting other monsters
In his Batman suit.

March 2010
Twins Eli and Sam are three years old

The Road to Fort Sumner

We drive into the wind
Off the eastern plains,
Bumping along a two-lane road
With ravens rising from their meal.

Through small towns,
No sign of life,
We pass homes of rock and mud
Crumbling back to dust.

Sandy side roads lead to ranches
Where black velvet cattle
Nibble on sparse grasses
In fields of scrub.

In this lonely desert land
Nothing seems to grow
More than two feet tall,
Defeated by the ceaseless winds.

This now seeming lifeless world
Once was home
To farms and railroad towns
Where historic tales unfolded,
And buried secrets
Of bygone days remain.

Destination Fort Sumner,
Along the Pecos River banks
Where Billy the Kid
Was taken by surprise and shot.
He now lies in a simple grave
Flanked by outlaw friends.

Here Navajo and Apache
Were forced into confinement,
Leaving their nomadic life
To become unwilling farmers.
Losing thousands
To starvation and disease
Before another long walk home.

Now their grief is remembered
At Bosque Redondo Memorial.
Their voices groan with sorrow
In the relentless wind,
As we follow their weary footsteps
Along the Pecos trail.

March 2010
Fort Sumner, New Mexico   **23**

Waiting for the Baby

I skirt pothole pools
Filled with last night's rain,
Now reflecting ponds
Of cloudless skies above.

My hand caresses
The silky tops
Of roadside grasses
As I head back
Along the track.

An early sun rises
Above a silhouette
Of jagged mountains
And warms my aging back.

I breathe the pure air,
While blue waves of flax
Nod to me
When I pass by
And wonder if
She will appear
On this Teton Valley
Summer day.

July 2009
Waiting for Margaret to arrive, Driggs, Idaho

Small Treasures

On a bookcase
A wooden wagon,
Pulled by Navajo clay horses,
Holds a cluster
Of tiny, horse-hair
Brazilian butterflies.

A glass wall case
Is filled with shells,
Miniature light houses,
Wooden docks and boats,
Painted seagulls, sand dollars,
Beach glass, and starfish
Recalling seashore holidays.

On the hearth
Multi-colored feathers,
Beaded and leather-tasseled,
Fan out and hold special memories
In a worn willow basket.

Toy bicycles
Of wire and metal
Race across a shelf.
And dolls from foreign lands
Parade on rows below.

Yet beaded bags,
Doll cradles,
Knife sheaths,
Leather gauntlets
Mounted on a wall
Hold ancient memories
Of people I will never know.

March 2010
Santa Fe

Oil Spill

Poetry should be of beauty,
Love, romance, and dreams.
But a tragedy may come
To be its muse,
No one greater
Than this careless blow
To our world
Beneath the sea.

An ugly headline,"Oil Spill"
We have read before.
But this may be the worst,
The yet untethered spill
 Is cruel and spreading
Along currents and tides.

It seeps into wetlands,
Deltas, coves and beaches,
Its oily blood
Spreading poison
To all life in its path.
Just as it seeps into
Our daily lives where
Workers stand idle
With the Gulf's bounty condemned.

The months are passing
The spill grows as it ages,
No end as yet forecast,
While a country which
Sends men to the moon
Seems helpless in its wake.

Someday it will be stopped,
But this sea world
Will be forever changed.
Generations yet to come,
Will have no memory
Of the beauty living there
"Once upon a time."

July 2010
Gulf of Mexico

Come Home Aubrey

Outside Fort Collins
In an empty field
Of high, dry grass,
Sits a large jagged rock
Painted pink.

Big blue letters plead
"Come Home Aubrey."

Is he far away
Fighting in a foreign land,
His days no longer
Filled with childhood games?

Perhaps he is
Straffing mountain sides
In a narrow canyon,
As his team seeks
The enemy hiding
Behind giant rocks
Like this one.

But those are
Painted red with blood.

28

August 2010
Fort Collins, Colorado

The Weavers of Las Golondrinas

Shearing
Washing
Carding
Spinning
Dying
Warping looms.

Year round
They sit together
Weaving, talking,
Sharing family stories
As they work the wool.

Sabanilla
Jerga
Colcha,
These weaving words
Intertwine
As they set
Spanish traditions
Into the wool.

Sitting across the placita
I hear the gentle hum
Of their voices harmonizing
Each week,
As their separate lives
Come together
To weave
For the love of wool.

October 2010
El Rancho de las Golondrinas, Santa Fe, New Mexico

Waiting for Work

On street corners
Across our land,
In the shelter of park or church,
They gather and wait
For hours or days,
Hands worn but skilled
In wood, brick and stone.
Each carries the story
That brought him north
Far from his birth land.

In my town
They gather at Guadalupe's sanctuary,
Heart of the unemployed.
Here they seek friendship
While they wait.

Today one stands alone.
On a sunny corner
Hatless, tall and dark,
His proud profile
Like that of a noble ancestor,
Oblivious to winters chill
But for hands pushed deep
Inside his thin coat pockets.

I want to know
What story brought him
From a far continent
To wait so patiently
For work in Santa Fe?

November 2010
Santuario de Guadalupe, Santa Fe

The Bookmark

Sitting in their study,
Reading a book
I looked around
To find a bookmark.

The desk was bare
Of paper scraps or string,
But on a shelf nearby
I saw a narrow card
Standing straight and new.

At its top
A small photo of
An old man smiling.
Below a faded figure
Of a young man
Stretching high,
Reaching for a ball.
Beside him the words
"Reach a little higher."

Who was this man?
Another famous author
Of whom I never heard,
But whose words
Sang to me?

It was sad to learn
That he had been their friend,
And this was his memorial card.

Christmas 2010
Chula Vista, California

EARTH CONNECTIONS

Winter Sunset

A late December afternoon
I head home
Into a fiery sunset.

Following the darkening road
I watch my windscreen
Fill with rainbow colors.

As the sun sets
Below the horizon
The reflection on the sky above
Becomes so brilliant
No painter could do it justice.

As my road fades
Into night,
The sky ahead
Stays full of color.

Blue and orange,
Reds and purples
Spread a winter palette
Behind a wash
Of thin gray clouds,
Wispy ribbons stretching
North to south.

This glory abruptly ended
Yet stayed for hours
Behind my eyes,
The perfect gift to day's end.

December 2008
Santa Fe, the road home

Tehachapi Pass

Driving east
Through moss-green foothills
We slice into the pass
Between snow-dusted
Brown and orange
Rounded peaks

In the late day light
They are like
Giant cupcakes
Frosted with sugar.

Climbing to the top,
The winter air
Comes cold and crisp
And mountain tops
Are now covered
In thick white icing.

Soon we are descending
Into a desert world
And leave Tehachapi's
Winter behind.

36

February 2009
Tehachapi Pass, California

Spring Green

When I grew up
Green was a word
To describe a color,
Like the greens
In my Crayola box:
Lime, Sea, and Emerald.

But no crayon green
Has ever matched
The green of buds
On the river trees
As I drive to work in Spring.

Green has other meanings.
Inexperience,
Renewal, or rebirth,
A fresh start.

But today
Green has become
A serious word
An icon for our environment,
Clean air and water.

It has become
A battle cry
Against pollution,
Deforestation,
Global warming.

It is a message of warning,
Our only chance
For survival
In the years ahead.

April 2009
Santa Fe

Summer Storm

This August afternoon
Clouds build up
Around the rim
Of our summer world.

Eastward
Anvil shapes stretch out
Above the Sangre Mountains.

Westward
Two giant fluffy snowmen
Wave their arms
And growl at me.

Does this mean relief
From the endless summer heat?
Or will they pass by
To leave us dry once more?

August 2009
Santa Fe

38

Forest Trail

Tire tracks mark
The narrow road
Filled with snowflakes,
A glittering uphill path
Between majestic pines.

On this clear, cold day
Of Christmas week,
A high Magritte moon sliver
Hangs on the deep blue
Of the afternoon sky.

My first day this year
On cross-country skis,
I struggle to regain
The graceful, gliding steps
Of younger years.

Along my flanks
Cotton balls of snow
Cling to gray branches
Of brush willows
And choke cherry bushes.

Frosted pines
Stretch tall and dark
Above me
As I ascend toward
Their embrace.

Shouts of children
Sledding below
Fade away
When I reach a silent meadow
Edged in shadows,
Deep in snow.

Alone and unafraid,
Unlike any "aloneness"
I have ever known,
I feel welcome to rest awhile
In this peaceful place
Before I turn and step
Inside my tracks
To return to family
And the world below.

Christmas 2009
Teton Foothills, Wyoming

40

January End of Days

My eastern horizon
Of gray velvet mountains
Iced in white
Spreads out before me
On the road to town.

The morning sun
Sihouettes their shapes,
While light and shadow
Define each foothill's
Mound, knob, and ridge
In sharp, black outline.

For days
This winter scene
Looms grand beyond compare,
Offering us
A gift of special beauty.

I shiver inside the car
And dream of spring.

January 2010
Santa Fe

In Between the Lines

Barefoot I walk
In between the lines.

I press my footprints
Into the smooth canvas
Of wet sand.

High tide line to my left,
Marked by rows of kelp
From morning's tide.

Low tide line to my right,
Touched by the lacy water's edge.
Our dog is framed
By a background
Of shinning, silver waves.

Along this undulating line
Clusters of small stones
Cast giant shadows,
Like miniature boulders.
Crab husks and
Broken mussel shells
Lie crumbling in wet sand.

Between the lines
My path is uncluttered,
Smooth and barren.
I walk, head down,
And search in vain
For unbroken treasures.

February 2010
Santa Barbara, California

The Garden

Still warm
Sunny days
Yet our garden
Warns of winter's coming.

Over the horizon
Cold, bitter January
Draws near.
The only month I fear.
A month of family loss
Down through the years.

Today
I feel warm
In autumn's sun
While trimming flowers
Whose time is done.

The clear nights
Are getting cold.
But geraniums,
Petunias and cosmos
Stay bright and cheer
Among the fallen leaves.

I cannot escape
The coming year
And frankly joyous
To still be here.

October 2010
Santa Fe

43

Pictures for Mom

"Being born in fall
Means the seasons unfold
In a special way for us."

My son's words
Introduce me
To an extraordinary gift,
A book of photos
Offering the seasons
In our personal order.

Through his photographic eye
I travel the seasons
Of our western states.
Fall, winter, spring and summer
Unfold pages of delight.

National parks to family gardens
Forest, mountains, lakes and streams,
Desert blooms and
The textured wood
Of ghost town shacks.

Falling autumn leaves,
Lichen encrusted rocks,
Ripe grapes
And rows of golden vines.

Trees encased in winter ice.
Snow-coated mountains,
Frozen drops
Suspended from a branch
Like a string of pearls.

Osprey and eagle
From high perches
Keep watch before
The nearing winter storm.

A tiny purple flower
Peeks from the shelter
Of a twisted root.
A stream's reflection
Mirrors the green leaves
Of a Napa Valley spring.

Fields of mountain lupine
And wild iris
Bring summer to the north,
While blossoms
Of all shapes and colors
Decorate our yards.

At the end,
Footprints travel the Pacific sands
Of an empty beach
And clouds stretching across
A broad Nevada sky
Leave shadow patterns
On a brown and vacant land.

In my gift
The beauties of our country
Are untouched by man.

November 2010
Photos from a book by Andy Berkenfield for my 75th Birthday

Christmas Road Trip

Day One

Leaving our stucco
Snug in its snowy blanket,
We drive south
On an empty Interstate,
Passing through a harsh, cold land.

The noon sun stretches
To its winter zenith,
Barely clearing the windshield.
Rusty dry grasses and
Black branched mesquite
Wave at us as we pass by.

Strange earthen mounds,
Like hidden pyramids
Holding ancient secrets,
Rise along our flanks.
We head into the loneliness
Of a quiet Sunday world
Toward a smooth blue sky
Arching over the border.
Through tiny Hatch,
Chili capital of the state
We turn toward the west.

More dull, flat land
Of wild winter grasses.
The tall stalks
Of giant yuccas
Bend under the weight
Of dry pods from summer's flowers.

Our narrow road
Cuts between low ridges
Whose dark silhouettes
Hold prehistoric profiles
Of reclining monsters.

Train tracks glisten in late sunlight
Waiting for the tremors
Of a west-bound freight
Whose stacked containers
Will flash their multi-colored sides.

Miles are market by power lines
Moving relentlessly westward
On their colossal legs.
They accompany us
To Lordsburg,
A dreary railroad town
Given a touch of color
By the fading sunset
As we settle for the night.

Day Two

Back once again on the Interstate
A straight "as an arrow" line into Arizona.
Joined now by speeding semis.
We climb through a series of rough ridges
Into the historic land of Cochise.
Texas Canyon's round boulders
Balance on each other's shoulders
Like a forest of strange totems
And other-worldly formations.

Susan sings "Perfect Day"
As we drive into Tombstone

To visit the neatly rowed graves
The final homes
Of historic outlaws
Murdered, hung, or killed by Indians.
Here no one lived
To die of old age.

Down through rolling ranchlands and
Golden grasslands
We touch the southern edge
Of the Mexican border
Before heading north
To Tubac's charms and mission history.
We come to rest in Green Valley
For a peaceful night.

Day Three

We begin at San Xavier del Bac
The 18th century monument
To Spanish missionary zeal
Still rising grandly
In the dusty Arizona desert.

Against dark rain clouds to the north,
It sparkles in the morning light.

Inside hundreds of angels and saints
Greet us in their faded colors,
While candles flicker
In the soft, ancient air.

A stop in Tucson
To embrace old friends
Getting frail,
Then back on the highway
Through flat, desert scrub.

Picacho Peak's sharp fins
Mark our entry into saguaro land.

Grey clouds close overhead
And the forecast rains begin.
We pierce a row of ragged ridges
Before descending toward Yuma.

Once again rows of trucks
Encase us with
Their metallic flanks,
Forming an endless chain
Of shiny links speeding westward.

It is time to stop and rest,
Take a deep breath
And find comfort
At a welcome inn.

Day Four

Our last day on the road.
Behind us clouds are breaking up,
So tempting to turn back
But family is waiting.
We head out of the desert
Into the rain and brooding clouds
Of California

Over the Valecito Mountains,
Rugged hills coated with
Layers of giant rocks
Like the topping on a crumb cake.
From sea level to four thousand feet
We climb in just minutes.

My hands grip the wheel,
Wipers whip back and forth
As we enter the fog and rain clouds
Trapped among the mountain peaks.
Other drivers speed by
In bewildering haste.
Why rush toward death,
It will come at its scheduled pace.

We descend to fields and farms,
Then the towns begin as
The road expands to five lanes
With interchanges and ramps
Overlapping in confusing curves.
We join the crazy
Crowd of cars and trucks
Traveling at top speed in driving rain.

At last it is time
To jump off this track
And calm our pace.
We have reached our family
And our Christmas destination.

December 2010
Santa Fe, New Mexico to Chula Vista, California

Alameda Seasons

In all seasons
Winding Alameda Road
Passes beneath
A lacy canopy
Of cottonwood branches
Sheltering our little river world.

Spring
The pale morning light
Brightens my day.
Trickling down through
Delicate green leaves
It dapples rocks and water
Rushing from mountain snow melt
To the Rio Grande.

Summer
The leaves have lost
Their freshness.
They droop, breathless
In the heavy sunshine.
A dusty hot sheen
Now filters through the leaves,
But their canopy still
Gives us welcome shade.

Autumn
Golden light falls gently
Through the canopy
Of multi-colored leaves
Which will soon blanket
The dry river bed
And pile along its banks.
With their dying
We sense an ending,
But the crisp morning air
Refreshes and helps me
Anticipate the coming winter.

Winter
The road is thick with snow
That also covers cottonwoods
Lined up like soldiers
To guard the river.
Their branches still lift high,
Entwining to give shelter
To the frozen world below.
The cold, pale sun
Casts dark patterns
On the snowy path
Where footprints are silent witness
To each chilly passerby.

2010
Santa Fe

PHOTO MEMORIES

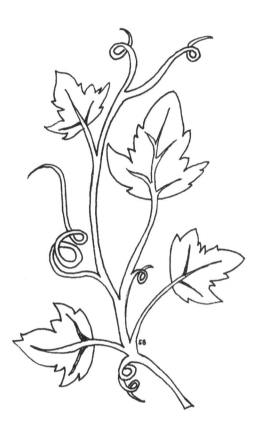

Sea of Flowers

She sits in a sea of flowers,
Daisies and wild iris
Stretching to the horizon,
With Eli, Sam and Maggie.

Like a mermaid
With her children
Rising from the deep,
They break through
The flowers' foam.

If there were a heaven
Where all was peace and beauty,
It should be
Like this field
Of white, blue, and green,
June's reward
For harsh, endless winters.

June 2010
Photo taken at Island Park, Idaho

The Valentine

White lilies
Dried blue asters
Surround a yellow rose.

This small bouquet,
Held snuggly
In a pewter vase
With scrolled handles,
Centers a lace doily
On a sky blue table.

Red wire hearts
Stand at attention
Announcing Valentine's Day.

Sixty five years old,
This gift
Will never fade.
It has been captured
In my grandmother's painting
That I may
Have my father
With me always.

56

July 2010
Santa Fe

Friendship

Three couples
Bound by years
Of raising children
In a foreign land,
Meet again to travel
In the West,
A different world
Dry, vast and spare.

Here we huddle close
Atop a sandstone mound
Against a bitter April wind
Laughing toward the lens,
Our grins a constant part
Of happy times together.

Though on the threshold
Of our sixties
We still looked so young,
In this photo
Taken years ago,
Posed between the Mitten Twins.

In spite of fading colors
It remains witness
To one of few shared memories
Since those early Paris years,
And as the colors pale
I doubt we will ever be
Together on that rock again.

October 2010
Monument Valley photo taken April 1993

A Summer Day

Here I am,
A child between
Father and brother,
All of us embedded
In a paperweight of glass.

We sit at dock's end,
Paul and I fascinated
By the precarious ash
Dangling off Dad's cigarette.

His white shirt sleeves
Are rolled neatly up
His sun-tanned arms.
Fishing pole leans close
Against a canvas pant leg.

An ancient crumpled hat,
A nest for hand-tied flies,
Rests beside him
On the weathered bench.

He looks deep in thought
Perhaps of the coming war
Or dreams unfulfilled,
Or the next fish to be caught?

A childhood memory
Is captured here
To sit upon my desk
Down through the years.

November 2010
Santa Fe, photo taken at Chautauqua Lake, New York in 1940

A Warm Day in November

I step outside
To sweep the brittle leaves
Still falling from
Our garden Aspens.
A late October frost
Has given way to sunny days.

The sun feels so warm
I sit down on the steps,
Turn my face upward
In defiance of skin cancer,
And tune out the day.

Shopping, cleaning,
Laundry, company coming,
All leave me
For a few quiet moments

Looking down
At my pale arms
Resting on my knees,
I think of the photo
Of you and I
On the front steps
Of our grey-shingled,
White-trimmed,
Slate-roofed home
"Back East."

Twenty six years younger
I sat in this same pose
In the heavy August heat
Of suburban New York,
With you and our first dog.
We had no thought
Of moving west one day.

November 2010
Santa Fe, photo on our steps in Hartsdale, New York 1984

AGING

Faux Spring

In the mirror
My pale face appears
An ancient mask.
The welcoming warmth
Of a March afternoon
Lures me outside
To sit on the steps.

From a shawl of illness,
Exhaustion is leaving.
Bed, meds and coughing
Are receding
As I unwind,
Stretch skyward,
Letting the sun
Penetrate my skin
And restore me.

Forgetting harmful rays
And my skin drying
Into parchment,
I crave this warmth
And feeling of rebirth.

The world is still.
No bees or breeze
Or rustling leaves.
My aging ears
A welcome barrier
To any sound.

I close my eyes.
I am on a beach,
Our children playing
At the shore line
My husband sleeping
By my side.

I open my eyes
To stare at the fountain
Still wrapped in its winter blanket
Of blue plastic,
Like a space ship
Resting in our garden.

The day's heat
Now inside me,
I don't care
If age spots spread,
Nothing is more healing
Than the sun's caress.

Pansies planted early,
In our impatience
To end the winter,
Might freeze tomorrow.
But today their colors
And cheerful faces
Encourage me.
I am recovering
And Spring is on its way.

March 2009
Santa Fe, in the garden

Remembering

When we met in spring
I, healing from heartbreak,
You celebrating life
After the army,
A handsome, penniless bachelor.

What strange chemistry
Brought us together,
A waspy Wellesley girl,
A skirt-chasing Jewish charmer?
We became so close
It hurt to be apart.
Do you remember?

My horizon only stretched
To our next weekend together.
Our idyll lasted to the autumn.

Forewarned from the day we met,
Still I was not ready
When you left to live your dream,
Waving from that toy Italian ship.

Through a blur of tears
I watched you wave
Over the heads of short Italians
Returning home
With their American treasures.

My horizon became infinite,
Uncertain.
Doubts of your return
Haunted my days and,
In spite of friends,
My lonely nights.

Tissue-thin blue air-letters
Arrived in profusion
A journal of your adventures
Through Europe and North Africa.
I carried them everywhere,
To feel connected.
To be a part of you.

Then some weeks of silence.
I knew you had found a friend.
My heart squeezed dry with jealousy
Until you resurfaced,
And we continued your journey.

One day, into my horizon
You stepped off a ship,
Gaunt and bearded
With your wanderlust
And dreams fulfilled.
I approached cautiously,
Uncertain of our future.

Gradually we joined
Comfortably together again
And began our years
Of marriage, children,
And shared travels.

Family years in France
Gave us added riches,
And on return
A first taste of the west
Nurtured a decision
To move to Santa Fe
More than twenty years ago.

Like the icing on the cake
Unexpected flowers,
The pleasure of a thoughtful gift,
This transition gave us
A new life, new friends
Who, with our growing family
Celebrate our long journey
In our home today.
.

May 28 2010
Fifty Year Anniversary, Santa Fe

Family Chain

In sickness and in health
We have lived
Through wars and peace,
Prosperity and hardship,
Part of a fading generation
Though not yet vanished.

At this anniversary
I gazed at grandchildren.
Which ones will I see graduate,
Marry, have children?
Will some remember us
Other than a faint memory
In a fading photograph?

As our world grows darker
We continue wars,
Abuse our land and seas.
May all our children
And their families
Meet challenges, have fun.
But may no war
Take any one of them.

When death do us part,
Memories of our parents
Go with us.
But our children
Will remember us
And theirs will continue
Our family chain.

June 2010
Santa Fe

Skin

Hummingbird shadows
Across the dawn lit window
Awaken me.

I look down
At my suntanned arm
Stretching along the sheet
Like a lazy lizard
Basking in the sun.

The lines and creases
Of my aging skin
Seem reptilian,
Reminiscent of photos
Of the crackling surface
Of a desert land.

As I rise to start the day
My bones and muscles
Send messages of pain,
Reminding me
That, inside my skin,
I am slowly melting.

September 2010
Santa Fe

View from a Hammock

A soft September day
No hint so far
Of coming winter.

I sway slightly
In their sagging hammock
Beneath aging trees.

Apples hang above me.
A cloudless sky
Is pierced by
The sharp, white silhouettes
Of cottonwoods.

A breeze so light
The leaves stay still.
Small birds
Dart between the trees
Like a school of fish
Flashing in the sunlight
As they turn in rhythm.

Pale butterflies
Skim among the scattered toys
Hiding in the tall grass.

It is the most perfect day
Of my 75th year.

September 2010
Tetonia, Idaho

Anniversary

This October day
Walking our son's wedding trail.
We breathe the alpine air
Of their mountain world
Amid the silent aspens
Now turning gold.

I think of eleven years
Of memories
Since this ritual,
Each one a milestone
In their lives and ours.

Like his brother and wife,
They are now blessed with children
And I feel blessed
To still be walking here,
While others
Have had to leave
Life's trail behind.

October 2010
Santa Fe, Sangre de Cristo Mountains

The Dinner Party

Four couples,
Comfortable old friends,
Sit around the table.

Conversation swings seamlessly,
Elections, baseball,
Grandchildren,
Jokes and travels,
Ailments, diet, exercise,
Work, music, art shows,
Back and forth
Until Don says
"How close are you to eighty?"

Suddenly quiet
We look at each other
And slowly say in turn
Two years, three, next month.

Nearing my seventy-fifth
I am surprised to be the youngest
In this ageless group
Of high achievers
Whose love of life
Belies their age.

October 30, 2010
Santa Fe

Secret Thoughts

Grace said it best,
We yearn for someone
With whom to share
Our secret thoughts.

Do you, like I
Have secret thoughts
Afraid to share?
Fears and wishes
We alone must bear,
No matter how dear
Our partner, child or friend.

I hold close my secret thoughts,
Lest I be misunderstood
When, in the clarifying,
Get tangled in the threads.

Even though grown men
With families of their own,
My mother self will worry
About my sons
Until the end.

Will their sons,
Now still young,
Have to fight in wars
When we are gone?

Will their daughters
Have lives full-filled,
With love and trust,
When we are dust?

I can't control
The world in which I live.
Why should I care
What happens later on?

Is this unexpected pain
A fatal sign?
Will I leave this world
In agony or peace?
So many friends
Already gone.
Who next will need release?

As my long life
Steps into autumn once again
I think of coming winter's
Cold arm around me
And already long
For spring's warm embrace.

I have no envy
Of those who share
Their secret thoughts
Through prayer.

But I seek relief that
I can feel,
A touch easing the tension
In my core.
A voice of understanding
At my side
That lets my tears release.

As I write these secret thoughts,
Sharing them with you
Is helping me
Find the comfort
That I seek.

October 2010
Santa Fe, New Mexico

CODA

77

Coda

The coda in book number one
Found me wondering
Who I might be
In the year 5003,
And would I remember
Being me.

The coda for book number two
Found me with a bike,
Apple green in hue.
I began to ride and have some fun
And realized life was not yet done.

Now here I am
Ending book number three
It may be my last conclusion.
What a redundancy!

I have had a lucky, love-filled life
Even in a world of strife.
And "never more"
Has not yet come.
So I can't vow
I'm really done.

January 2011
Santa Fe

(Coda means "tail" in Italian and is the concluding
passage for a musical composition.)

CPSIA information can be obtained
at www.ICGtesting.com
Printed in the USA
BVHW041415260423
663002BV00008B/689

9 780865 348271